Original title:
Happiness Blueprint

Author: Clement Portlander
ISBN HARDBACK: 978-9916-88-218-4
ISBN PAPERBACK: 978-9916-88-219-1

The Book of Bright Affections

In pages filled with laughter bright,
Tender whispers softly light.
Every moment, a treasured glance,
We dance together, lost in chance.

A tapestry of hearts entwined,
Love's gentle hand forever kind.
With every word, a spark ignites,
In this book, our joy delights.

Mapping Joy's Pathway

A compass formed of dreams and grace,
Guides us through this sacred space.
With every step, our spirits soar,
Unlocking joy behind each door.

The path is strewn with laughter's song,
Where every right feels just as wrong.
We chart our course through sun and rain,
In joy's embrace, we feel no pain.

The Recipe for Radiant Living

A pinch of love and joy combined,
Stirred with kindness, perfectly aligned.
Add a sprinkle of laughter's cheer,
Bake with passion, year by year.

Savor moments, warm and bright,
Seasoned well with pure delight.
A dash of dreams to light our way,
In this recipe, we choose to stay.

The Enchantment of Everyday Delights

In morning's light, the world awakes,
With tiny wonders, joy partakes.
A blossom's bloom, a child's sweet laugh,
Moments woven on joy's behalf.

Each sunset paints the sky anew,
Magic found in every hue.
In simple things, our hearts unite,
Everyday delights, pure and bright.

The Alchemy of Light and Laughter

In shadows bright, the laughter sings,
Transforming dark with vibrant wings.
A spark ignites within the night,
Where joy and hope take wondrous flight.

Through golden rays, our spirits bloom,
Dispelling doubt, dispelling gloom.
Each chuckle, a potion, warm and clear,
A symphony of love we hold dear.

The Seeds of Positive Tomorrows

With every seed that we now plant,
A future bright, we boldly chant.
Watered by dreams and tender care,
Hope takes root in the vibrant air.

The sun will shine on paths we tread,
As every word of kindness spreads.
Together we'll weave tomorrow's thread,
In a tapestry of joy ahead.

Murmurs of Blissful Dreams

In the quiet night, dreams softly call,
Whispers of magic that cradle all.
Stars above twinkle with delight,
As hearts entwine in the moonlit night.

Each sigh a wish, each pulse a song,
Guiding our spirits where we belong.
Murmurs of bliss, like a gentle breeze,
Cradle our hopes, setting them at ease.

A Serenade to Simple Joys

In morning light, the laughter flows,
Like soft, sweet petals of budding rose.
A friendly smile, a gentle glance,
In simple things, we find our chance.

Moments cherished, small and bright,
Glow like stars in the velvet night.
A serenade, these joys we sing,
In every heart, let happiness spring.

Sunbeams in the Shadow

In the hush of twilight's grace,
Quiet whispers find their place.
Gold-lit edges softly gleam,
Hope ignites like a fading dream.

Flickers dance on dusky ground,
Laughter lost will soon be found.
Shadows stretch as light does fade,
In the dark, new paths are laid.

Crafting Clouds of Contentment

Fluffy forms in skies of blue,
Wanderers dance, as breezes do.
Each puff a dream, a gentle sigh,
Beneath, the world seems to fly high.

Cotton dreams drift slow and light,
Soft as whispers in the night.
Hope unfurls in the air,
Crafting joys beyond compare.

The Map of Lively Spirits

Every heart a winding road,
Travel far, shed off the load.
Together on this journey's path,
We share our dreams, escape the wrath.

Markers of joy in every mile,
Unfolding tales that make us smile.
Guided by the stars that shine,
In this dance, your heart is mine.

Portraits of Everyday Joy

In the morning's golden light,
Simple moments feel so bright.
Children laugh in wild delight,
Painting life in colors right.

Tea cups clink in gentle cheer,
Whispers shared, the heart draws near.
Every glance a story told,
In these frames, love's warmth unfolds.

Crafting a Symphony of Smiles

In twilight's glow, we find our tune,
Soft laughter floats, a sweet balloon.
Notes of joy, like fireflies dart,
Each smile a rhythm, a beating heart.

We gather dreams, let worries fade,
In harmony, our spirits laid.
With every chord, the world aligns,
Crafting peace within the signs.

Building Bridges of Bliss

Over rivers deep, our hearts connect,
Hand in hand, we build, reflect.
With bricks of love, we span the gap,
Creating pathways, a warm map.

The laughter shared, a sturdy beam,
In the light, we find our dream.
Each step we take, a story told,
Bonds of bliss, forever bold.

The Architecture of Elation

With beams of hope, we raise the sky,
Each moment captured, a sweet sigh.
Walls adorned with laughter's hue,
Foundations strong, built for two.

Inspired by dawn, designs unfold,
Creating wonders that shine like gold.
In every corner, joy's embrace,
A sanctuary, our happy place.

Whispers of Contentment

Soft whispers dance upon the breeze,
In quiet corners, hearts find ease.
Petals fall, like gentle sighs,
In nature's arms, true bliss resides.

A tender touch, a knowing glance,
In simple moments, we find our chance.
Contentment's song, a lullaby,
In peaceful nights, our spirits fly.

Navigating the Seas of Serenity

On tranquil waves, our boat does glide,
With whispers soft, the winds confide.
The horizon calls, a distant blue,
In peace we sail, with skies so true.

The sun dips low, a golden hue,
Each moment breathes, fresh and anew.
In silent depths, our dreams reside,
Together we drift, side by side.

The stars emerge, a twinkling guide,
Through darkened nights, they never hide.
With hearts aligned, we chart our way,
In harmony, we'll find our sway.

The Framework of Positive Futures

In sturdy frames, our hopes take shape,
Each vision drawn, a vibrant drape.
With every thought, we build our dreams,
A tapestry of hopeful themes.

Together we lay, each brick with care,
In unity strong, we shall prepare.
With colors bright, we paint the day,
In the light of love, our path will sway.

The future's light, it shines so clear,
With every step, we conquer fear.
Together we rise, on wings of trust,
In nurturing bonds, in hope we must.

Vistas of Exuberance

From mountain tops, the valleys sing,
With laughter bright, the joys they bring.
In fields of gold, let spirits soar,
With nature's grace, we long for more.

The flowers bloom, a joyful dance,
Their colors burst, they take a chance.
In every petal, life's song plays,
In simple moments, love displays.

The sunlit streams, they gleam with glee,
In every ripple, wild and free.
With open hearts, we chase delight,
In every glance, the world feels right.

The Palette of Playfulness

With brushes wide, we splash the scene,
In joyful strokes, we paint the dream.
With laughter bright, our colors blend,
In every hue, we find a friend.

From playful hearts, the art unfolds,
In canvases, our life beholds.
With every swirl, the joy cascades,
In simple games, our fears must fade.

Let's dance with shadows, leap with light,
In every moment, pure delight.
With hearts aglow, we twirl and spin,
In the world of play, let life begin.

Threads of Tranquil Tapestry

In the quiet dawn of day,
Soft whispers of light play,
Colors blend, a gentle hue,
Nature's peace, a heart anew.

Woven stillness, threads entwined,
Moments cherished, heart aligned,
Every stitch a tale to tell,
In this calm, we weave so well.

Breezes hum a soothing song,
In this place where we belong,
A tapestry of dreams takes flight,
In the embrace of twilight's light.

Peaceful hours, softly glide,
In the fabric, hope resides,
Through each thread, our spirits lift,
A tranquil world, our greatest gift.

The Chronicles of a Joyful Journey

From the start, when dreams arise,
Underneath the endless skies,
Steps we take, both bold and bright,
Every path leads to delight.

Through the valleys, hills we climb,
Glimmers of joy, passing time,
Every laugh, a treasure found,
In the journey, joy abounds.

Friendship blooms along the way,
Guiding hearts, come what may,
With each turn, new wonders greet,
In this dance, our lives complete.

As the stars begin to gleam,
We reflect on every dream,
Chronicles of joy unfold,
In our hearts, the tales retold.

The Diary of Blissful Days

In the pages of sunlight,
Every moment feels just right,
Laughter echoes, softly rings,
In my heart, the joy it brings.

Morning dew on blades of grass,
Whispers of time, how they pass,
Each hour, a cherished embrace,
In this place, I find my grace.

Evenings soft, with fading light,
Stars appear, a wondrous sight,
Writing tales of golden rays,
In the diary of blissful days.

Gratitude in every line,
Each small joy, purely divine,
For the love that fills the air,
In this life, we find our share.

The Codex of Carefree Dreams

In the depths of twilight's glow,
Whispers of the night bestow,
Carefree hearts, like birds in flight,
Chasing dreams in soft moonlight.

Unwritten pages, tales unfold,
Magical journeys to behold,
In each dream, our spirits soar,
Opening wide, the unseen door.

Clouds of wonder gently drift,
Through the sky, our thoughts uplift,
In the codex, secrets greet,
Maps of dreams, so wild and sweet.

Every night a brand new quest,
In our hearts, we find our rest,
Let the stars guide where we roam,
In carefree dreams, we find our home.

Garden of Sunlit Dreams

In the hush of morning light,
Petals dance and spirits rise,
Whispers of the dawn ignite,
Nature's song beneath the skies.

Breezes play on silken leaves,
Colors bloom in joyful sway,
In this peace, the heart believes,
Magic weaves through every day.

Butterflies in gentle flight,
Gathering nectar, sweet and pure,
Every moment feels so bright,
In this garden, hearts endure.

As the sun begins to fade,
Evenings hum a lullaby,
In our dreams, love is remade,
In this haven, we can fly.

Foundations of a Radiant Soul

In the depths of quiet thought,
Roots of joy begin to grow,
Lessons learned and battles fought,
Building strength that we can show.

Through the storms that test our will,
We find peace in every scar,
As we climb each daunting hill,
Learning who we truly are.

Threads of hope will intertwine,
In the fabric of our days,
With each heartbeat, we refine,
Glowing in the light's embrace.

In the mirror, there we find,
Reflections of a journey bold,
Foundations of a heart aligned,
Radiant stories to be told.

Glimmers of Laughter

In the warmth of friendly eyes,
Laughter bubbles, bright and clear,
Moments shared, both low and high,
In each chuckle, we feel near.

From the silly to the sweet,
Every smile a treasure made,
As we gather, hearts repeat,
Joyful sounds that never fade.

With each joke that lights the room,
Memories begin to spark,
Chasing shadows, pushing gloom,
In the dawn, we leave a mark.

In the echoes of our play,
Glimmers shine like stars above,
Every laugh, a bright bouquet,
In each heart, we share the love.

Chasing Traces of Ecstasy

In the chase of fleeting dreams,
We find magic in the night,
Every whisper softly beams,
Guiding souls towards the light.

Moments swirl like autumn leaves,
Carried by the winds of fate,
In the laughter, our heart cleaves,
To the joy that we create.

Through the shadows, we will roam,
Seeking treasures yet unseen,
In each heartbeat, we find home,
In the dance, a vibrant sheen.

Chasing traces of delight,
In the rhythm, we belong,
In the ebb of day and night,
Life's a fleeting, joyous song.

The Canvas of Joy

Brush strokes of laughter dance wide,
Colors of love softly glide.
In this art, I'm free to play,
Creating my bright, joyful day.

Every hue tells a story bold,
Of friendships cherished, dreams of old.
With each touch, a smile grows,
In the canvas of joy, my heart glows.

Splashes bright of hope and cheer,
Amidst the shadows, love draws near.
Here, in this space, I vividly see,
The masterpiece that is me.

In every detail, beauty found,
In the silence, laughter's sound.
The canvas of joy, ever bright,
Guides my heart to pure delight.

Threads of Light

Golden threads weave through the day,
Binding moments in gentle sway.
Threads of laughter, silk of dreams,
In every stitch, a story beams.

Glistening strands in twilight's hue,
Intertwined, me and you.
With every heartbeat, we ignite,
A tapestry woven with threads of light.

In shadows dark, they softly gleam,
Binding our hopes like a shared dream.
With each woven line, we find,
A connection that's beautifully blind.

Together we walk, hand in hand,
Through the soft arcs, a bright strand.
Threads of light, forever entwined,
In the fabric of love, we are defined.

Whispers of Contentment

In the silence, soft whispers flow,
Gentle secrets that only we know.
Contentment lingers in the air,
A tranquil heart, a soothing prayer.

Moments cherished, quiet and true,
In simple joys, just me and you.
The world fades, we breathe in deep,
In whispers of contentment, we keep.

As stars twinkle in the night sky,
Under their glow, worries fly.
Wrapped in warmth of the evening's grace,
In every sigh, I find my place.

Together, we paint the night's charm,
In each other's embrace, safe and warm.
Whispers of contentment softly sing,
In the quiet, my heart takes wing.

The Art of Serene Days

In morning light, the world awakes,
Softly cradling the dawn that breaks.
The canvas spreads, calm and clear,
A serene day waiting near.

Birdsongs weave through the gentle breeze,
Nature's lullabies, sweet with ease.
Every moment flows like a stream,
In the art of living, we dream.

With each passing hour, peace unfolds,
In whispers of stories yet untold.
Time slows down in this gentle haze,
Crafting the art of serene days.

As the sun dips low, colors ignite,
A masterpiece painted in twilight's light.
In every breath, serenity plays,
In the rhythm of these serene days.

Chasing the Sunbeam

In morning light we rise and run,
Chasing dreams like a golden sun.
With laughter bright and spirits high,
Each moment glimmers, we soar and fly.

Through fields of hope, we dance and play,
Finding magic in every ray.
The world is vivid, colors swell,
In sunbeam's embrace, all is well.

We weave the day with threads of gold,
In stories shared, new paths unfold.
With every step, we leave a trace,
Chasing the light, in love's warm grace.

Windows to Wondrousness

Peering through panes of glass so clear,
Each window shows a world we hold dear.
Stories flicker in the glint of light,
Inviting us to journeys of delight.

Time drifts softly like a gentle breeze,
Through open windows, our hearts find ease.
In shadows cast, new dreams ignite,
Wondrousness awaits in every sight.

With hands outstretched, we reach for more,
Through these portals, we explore.
Moments linger like whispers sweet,
In every view, our lives complete.

The Blueprint of Bright Tomorrows

On pages blank, we sketch our dreams,
A blueprint formed by hopeful schemes.
With vibrant colors, futures gleam,
In the heart's design, we dare to dream.

Building towers with love's embrace,
Every challenge a chance to trace.
Foundations strong, we rise and grow,
In the light of faith, we choose to flow.

With every line, we craft our fate,
A vision bold that can't be late.
In united steps, we pave the way,
For bright tomorrows, we chase today.

Patterns of Peace and Joy

In gentle waves, the moments blend,
Patterns of peace on hearts depend.
Each breath a gift, so pure and bright,
In stillness found, we feel the light.

Laughter ripples through quiet air,
Joy's tender touch is everywhere.
With every smile, we sow the seeds,
Of love and kindness, the heart needs.

In harmony, we walk the path,
Creating beauty in nature's bath.
Patterns of joy, in every hue,
A tapestry woven from me and you.

The Geometry of Smiles

In the corners where laughter lies,
Curved edges of a joyful surprise.
Angles meeting with hearts so light,
Creating patterns that shine so bright.

Each grin draws a line to connection,
A point of warmth, pure affection.
Shapes entwined in a moment's grace,
A masterpiece carved on each face.

In every smile, a story unfolds,
Echoes of warmth in the world it holds.
Geometric wonders in fleeting frames,
A universe spun from simple names.

Together we sketch with joy between,
Lines of friendship, soft and serene.
In the geometry of smiles we find,
The art of living, beautifully designed.

A Tapestry of Glowing Moments

Threads of laughter weave through time,
Each glowing encounter, a subtle rhyme.
Colors blend in a vibrant array,
Painting memories that never fray.

In a glance shared across a room,
In gentle whispers, love's sweet bloom.
Every moment stitched with care,
A tapestry rich, beyond compare.

Sunset hues and dawn's warm light,
Wrap our souls in pure delight.
Each thread counts as we weave our fate,
Binding hearts with love innate.

Together we craft this intricate art,
A tapestry strong, never to part.
Embracing all, the moments we hold,
In the glow of now, rich and bold.

The Symphony of Well-Being

A gentle breeze carries soft notes,
In harmony where happiness floats.
Strings of laughter, percussion of joy,
Life's sweetest song, never to destroy.

Chords of kindness resonate deep,
In the hearts where love weaves and leaps.
Melodies of peace, so soothing and clear,
Compose a rhythm that draws us near.

With every breath, we dance in tune,
Under the glow of the silver moon.
The symphony swells as we sing along,
Orchestrating life, our everlasting song.

Together we sway, our spirits align,
In this precious moment, you are mine.
In the symphony of well-being we find,
A melody pure, both heart and mind.

Fragments of Joy in Everyday Life

In a morning glow, sunlight spills,
Over dew-kissed grass, a heart that thrills.
Simple pleasures in every sight,
Fragments of joy, sparkling light.

A child's laugh echoes in the air,
Moments like these, beyond compare.
In quiet corners, happiness sings,
Finding delight in the smallest things.

With every breath, a chance to pause,
To soak in wonder without a cause.
Each fragment gathered, cherished and bright,
A mosaic of light, ever so right.

In the rush of life, let us not miss,
The little treasures wrapped in bliss.
For joy resides in the everyday strife,
A tapestry woven, our beautiful life.

The Treasure Hunt for Everyday Miracles

Amidst the rush, we pause to see,
The simple joys that set us free.
A warm cup held in tender hands,
A stranger's smile, like sunlit sands.

Whispers of leaves in the gentle breeze,
The laughter shared beneath the trees.
A child's delight, a dog's quick chase,
In every moment, find a trace.

A rainbow after storms have passed,
The fleeting glow, a sunset cast.
In tiny sparks and fleeting sights,
Miracles dance in daily lights.

So treasure these, both small and grand,
For life's true wealth is always planned.
Each day a map, each hour a clue,
The hunt for joy begins with you.

The Journey to Joyful Spaces

Step by step, we wander near,
Through fields of hope, we shed our fear.
With open hearts and open minds,
The path unfolds, the light it finds.

In laughter's echo, spirits soar,
In every glance, we see much more.
The beauty found in simple things,
Awakens joy that singing brings.

A gentle breeze, a painted sky,
The clouds that drift, the birds that fly.
Together, we embrace the view,
In every step, a journey true.

So cherish moments, brave and bold,
In each new space, a story told.
With every turn, adventure calls,
In joyful spaces, our spirit enthralls.

The Art of Joyful Living

In morning light, our canvas spreads,
With colors bright, and thoughts like threads.
Each day a stroke of vibrant hue,
Creating joy in all we do.

With laughter loud and kindness shared,
With open hearts, we show we cared.
The art of living, bold and free,
Is found in shared connectivity.

In whispered dreams and hopeful sighs,
In every tear that softly dries.
We paint our lives with every choice,
And in our hearts, we find our voice.

So gather shades, both light and dark,
For every moment leaves a mark.
With brush in hand, let's shape our way,
In the art of living, come what may.

The Color Palette of Delight

In twilight's glow, the colors blend,
With pinks and purples, life transcends.
Each hue a note, each shade a song,
In this wild world, we all belong.

A splash of red, like love's embrace,
A dash of green, time's gentle trace.
The golden yellows start the day,
While blues of twilight softly play.

In every shade, a story waits,
In sunlit fields, in open gates.
The palette rich, the strokes so bright,
In every corner, pure delight.

So paint with joy, let colors flow,
In life's great canvas, let us grow.
Together, let's create our art,
With every heartbeat, every start.

Harmonizing Heartbeats

In the quiet of the night,
Two souls dance, hearts in flight.
Rhythm whispers, soft and sweet,
As they move to their own beat.

Beneath the stars, a gentle glow,
Together they weave, love's flow.
Each pulse a note, strong and clear,
In this symphony, they hold dear.

With every breath, they synchronize,
A melody that never dies.
Hands entwined in perfect grace,
In this moment, time can't erase.

As dawn arrives, the song remains,
In heartbeats lost, joy sustains.
Harmony found in every sigh,
Together forever, you and I.

The Canvas of Cheery Souls

Brushstrokes of laughter fill the air,
Colors vibrant, a world so rare.
Every smile a joyful shade,
In the sun's warmth, dreams are laid.

With every stroke, a story told,
Of friendship bright, and love so bold.
Painted skies in hues of hope,
In this art, we learn to cope.

Splashes of kindness, gentle rain,
Washing away all doubts and pain.
On this canvas, hearts collide,
Creating beauty, side by side.

Each moment captured, pure and true,
A masterpiece made just for you.
In the gallery of life, we share,
The canvas brightens, joy laid bare.

The Odyssey of Optimism

With sails unfurled, we set to roam,
A journey bright, we call it home.
Through tempests fierce and skies so blue,
Our hearts remain steadfast and true.

Each wave a challenge, fierce and bold,
Yet in our eyes, a tale unfolds.
Together we'll weather every storm,
With hopeful hearts, we stay warm.

The compass points to realms unknown,
In every step, we have grown.
Chasing dreams on horizons wide,
In our spirits, hope will abide.

As stars align on the midnight sea,
The odyssey shapes who we're meant to be.
With every dawn, our dreams we'll greet,
In a dance of life, our hearts will meet.

Reflections in a Joyous Mirror

In the glass, what do we see?
Glimmers of happiness, wild and free.
Each smile shines, a radiant glow,
In vibrant colors, our spirits flow.

Echoes of laughter fill the space,
Moments cherished, love's embrace.
As we gaze, our dreams align,
In joyous reflections, we brightly shine.

Through every trial, brightly we rise,
In the mirror's depth, no disguise.
With every glance, we support and cheer,
In this journey, our hearts draw near.

So let's celebrate the light we share,
In reflections of joy, we lay bare.
With every smile, we find our place,
In this mirror of love, we find our grace.

Fragments of Flickering Joy

In twilight's glow, the whispers dance,
Soft laughter spills, a fleeting glance.
The echoes of dreams, they intertwine,
In every heart, a spark divine.

Moments woven, fragile and bright,
Like stars that shimmer in the night.
Holding close what time may steal,
Each fragment a treasure, our joy reveals.

In simple places, joys arise,
In shared secrets and wide-eyed sighs.
Though shadows loom and shadows play,
We gather each fraction and find our way.

Let not the world dim our spark,
For every smile ignites a mark.
With open hearts, we can explore,
These flickering fragments forevermore.

The Spectrum of Satisfied Souls

A canvas painted with hues so bright,
Every shade whispers, love's delight.
In laughter's warmth, we find our place,
With every smile, a soft embrace.

From deep ocean blue to sunset gold,
Stories in colors, gently told.
Hearts intertwined, in rhythm they sing,
A harmony born from simple things.

Each soul a color, uniquely defined,
In this spectrum, true joy we find.
Dancing together, as moments unfold,
In the tapestry of life, bright and bold.

Through trials and triumphs, we paint anew,
In the gallery of existence, we'll break through.
Together we flourish, a joyful role,
Embracing each other, the spectrum of soul.

The Legacy of Laughter

In echoes of joy, we weave our tale,
Through giggles and roars, we shall prevail.
A legacy born in shared delight,
Carried on wings of day and night.

Through ups and downs, our spirits soar,
Laughter, the key to every door.
In silly moments and silly rhymes,
We find our happiness, lost in time.

In circles of friends, we find our way,
With every chuckle, here we stay.
In tears of joy, we unearth our worth,
A legacy of laughter, abundant mirth.

So let us echo, let us cheer,
For laughter shared, so precious, dear.
Together we'll build a warm embrace,
In this legacy, we find our place.

Seeds of Splendor

In gardens of dreams, we plant our seeds,
With whispers of hope, we nurture our needs.
Watered with love, sunlight, and care,
The splendor of life blooms everywhere.

Each petal unfurls, a story to tell,
In the dance of the breezes, we flourish well.
Roots intertwine, in soil so rich,
A tapestry woven, every stitch.

Through trials of winter, through storms we grow,
With patience and faith, the blossoms show.
Dreams that take flight, in colors so bold,
Seeds of splendor, a vision to hold.

In every heartbeat, in every embrace,
We cultivate beauty, our shared space.
Together we'll nurture, together we'll thrive,
In the garden of life, our spirits alive.

The Melody of Merriment

In the heart of laughter's dance,
Joy unfolds with every glance.
Notes of happiness softly play,
Melodies brightening the day.

Friends gather round in warm embrace,
Smiles spreading on every face.
Echoes of fun fill the air,
A symphony that eases care.

Moments cherished, simple and sweet,
Every heartbeat a rhythmic beat.
Swaying gently in life's song,
Where all souls truly belong.

Let us cherish this vibrant tune,
Beneath the sun, beneath the moon.
Together we sing, hearts align,
In the melody, our spirits shine.

A Symphony of Sweetness

Sugar-spun dreams dance in the air,
Whispers of love linger everywhere.
Candied laughter, a joyful sound,
Unity in sweetness is found.

Soft notes of kindness bring us near,
In every heartbeat, we feel sincere.
A sweet serenade fills our hearts,
Binding us closely, never apart.

Moments of bliss, like honey dripped,
In the warmth of friendship, we are equipped.
With every smile, a story is told,
A timeless bond, more precious than gold.

A symphony of flavors so bright,
Life's sweetest moments take flight.
We create a chorus, pure and true,
In this harmony, we start anew.

The Codex of Cheerful Encounters

In the book of laughter, pages turn,
Each encounter, a lesson to learn.
Stories woven, thread by thread,
In the hearts of joy, they are spread.

Faces bright, illuminated cheer,
Friendship's embrace always near.
Whimsical tales we share with glee,
In this codex, we are free.

Moments captured, forever to stay,
Golden memories lead the way.
In every chapter, a spark ignites,
Cheerful moments, sweet delights.

Let's write our tale with colors bold,
In this codex, our stories unfold.
Together we dance, together we sing,
In joyful encounters, love takes wing.

The Design of Dreamers

Upon the canvas of the night,
Dreamers gather, hearts alight.
Stars are visions, glimmering bright,
Painting the world in hues of light.

Whispers of hope, a gentle breeze,
Carrying dreams with such ease.
In this design, futures intertwine,
Woven together, hearts align.

Every vision crafted with care,
A tapestry vibrant beyond compare.
With every heartbeat, we aspire,
Igniting within a sacred fire.

Let's chase the dawn with spirits high,
In the sky, our dreams shall fly.
Together we'll create, uncover schemes,
In the grand design of our dreams.

The Voyage to Elated Horizons

A ship of dreams upon the sea,
With sails that whisper, wild and free.
The stars above, our guiding light,
We chase the dawn, dispelling night.

Waves of wonder crash and sing,
Every heartbeat, joy they bring.
With every swell, we rise and fall,
Together bound, we heed the call.

Through storms and squalls, we steer ahead,
In trust and hope, we're gently led.
Our spirits soar, horizons wide,
In this grand journey, we abide.

Elated shores await our feet,
In the horizon, dreams complete.
With open hearts, we will embrace,
The voyage now, our sacred space.

The Spirits of Gentle Laughter

In twilight's glow, the soft winds play,
With giggles shared, we drift away.
Beneath the trees, we weave our cheer,
The spirits dance, our joy sincere.

With every word, a melody,
In laughter's arms, we're wild and free.
Together close, in warmth we find,
A bond unbroken, heart entwined.

In gentle echoes, we reside,
Where happiness and love collide.
Their whispers weave a magic air,
In every chuckle, strength we share.

As evening falls, the stars will gleam,
We hold on tight to this sweet dream.
In laughter's light, our spirits soar,
United always, evermore.

Embracing Sunlit Moments

A golden glow on morning's dew,
With every ray, a spark anew.
In open fields, we laugh and play,
Soaking in warmth, the perfect day.

Each fleeting hour, a treasure brief,
In nature's arms, we find our relief.
With skies of blue, we dance in glee,
Embracing life, wild and free.

The world, a canvas bright and bold,
In sunlit moments, stories told.
With every breath, we share our dreams,
In the light of love, nothing redeems.

As twilight fades, the colors blend,
Our hearts aglow, a joyful send.
In memories made, forever stay,
Embracing sunlit moments play.

The Sanctuary of Sweet Serenity

In quiet corners, shadows blend,
A refuge found where troubles end.
With nature's breath, our spirits heal,
In sacred space, we learn to feel.

The whispering leaves, a gentle song,
In harmony, we all belong.
With every sigh, worries dissolve,
The peace within, we then resolve.

Among the blossoms, calm resides,
With open hearts, the world abides.
In moments still, we find our grace,
A sanctuary, our perfect place.

As starlit skies unfold the night,
We bask in all that feels so right.
In sweet serenity, love will reign,
A warm embrace, forever plain.

The Map to Inner Sunshine

In the heart where whispers dwell,
Paths of gold and stories swell.
Every step a ray of light,
Guiding dreams through darkest night.

A compass drawn with love and care,
Moments cherished, moments rare.
With each breath, the journey flows,
A map unfolds where kindness grows.

Through valleys deep and mountains high,
The inner sun will never die.
In shadows cast, we find the way,
Shining bright, come what may.

So trust the journey deep inside,
Where joy and peace together reside.
Follow where the heart leads true,
The map to sun is drawn for you.

Designs of Pure Joy

In colors bright, the canvas shows,
A dance of life where laughter grows.
Every stroke, a memory made,
Woven in sunshine, never to fade.

Threads of silver, gold, and blue,
Intertwined with love so true.
Crafted dreams in playful sway,
Designs of joy light up the day.

With every heartbeat, joy expands,
An artful touch from gentle hands.
The fabric soft, the patterns free,
In pure delight, we find the key.

So let your spirit paint the sky,
Embrace the wonder, let it fly.
In life's grand tapestry, we play,
Designs of joy, come out and play.

The Garden of Serene Moments

In quiet corners, shadows blend,
A garden blooms where time can mend.
Whispers of the leaves so dear,
Serene moments draw us near.

With every petal, peace awakes,
In emerald paths where silence takes.
The heart finds solace, soft and wide,
In tranquil spaces where dreams abide.

Butterflies dance on gentle breeze,
Nature's song brings sweet unease.
In the hush of dusk's embrace,
We discover our sacred place.

So walk among the fragrant blooms,
Let go of all your worldly glooms.
In this garden, feel the flow,
Of serene moments, sweet and slow.

Tapestry of Laughter

Threads of joy in colors bright,
Woven tales in soft moonlight.
Each giggle like a starry thread,
A tapestry where love is spread.

In every corner, warmth abounds,
Laughter echoes, joy resounds.
With every smile, a story spins,
In this fabric, the heart begins.

Gathered friends in playful cheer,
Moments cherished, always near.
The threads of laughter joyful weave,
In every heart, we dare believe.

So let the laughter fill the air,
A world of joy, beyond compare.
In this tapestry, life unravels,
With laughter's touch, our spirits travel.

The Legacy of Laughter and Light

In the whisper of dawn, joy awakes,
Echoes of laughter, the heart gently shakes.
Sunbeams dance on laughter's sweet face,
Memories woven, a warm, tender embrace.

In the shadows of night, stories unfold,
With each shared smile, a treasure untold.
Laughter like echoes, bright and so bold,
Casting away darkness, like threads of fine gold.

With each passing moment, we gather and share,
An orchestra played, with love in the air.
Laughter's the music, our spirits ignite,
A legacy crafted in laughter and light.

In the cradle of time, let echoes resound,
The legacy of laughter forever unbound.
With hearts intertwined, our joy takes flight,
In a world full of laughter, we shine ever bright.

Emblems of Ecstatic Existence

In gardens of dreams, vibrant and free,
Life twirls and dances, a jubilant spree.
Colors collide, like hearts that unite,
Each moment a gem, a spark of pure light.

In whispers of breezes, joy finds its song,
A chorus of laughter that carries us along.
With each step we take, we paint our own fate,
Emblems of living, where love resonates.

In the warmth of the sun, in the cool evening breeze,
Every heartbeat signifies joy's sweetest tease.
Living the moment, embracing the now,
Ecstatic existence, we pledge and we vow.

Through valleys and peaks, let our spirits soar,
In this ecstasy, we forever explore.
With souls intertwined and visions so bright,
We gather like stars, in the canvas of night.

Fertile Fields of Joyful Encounters

In fields of green where the wildflowers sway,
Joyful encounters light up the day.
Hearts bloom like petals, vibrant and bright,
In the dance of connection, spirits take flight.

Every smile exchanged, a seed gently sown,
In the garden of friendship, together we've grown.
With laughter as rain, our spirits we share,
In these fertile fields, love blossoms with care.

Underneath the vast sky, we gather and sing,
United in joy, through the warmth that we bring.
With every heart touched, each moment we cherish,
In this realm of connection, no joy can perish.

Together we weave our stories of cheer,
In the tapestry of life, so vibrant, so clear.
Fertile fields await, filled with love's sweet embrace,
In joyful encounters, we find our true place.

The Atlas of Contented Souls

In the quiet of twilight, we gather as one,
Contented souls shining, our journey begun.
Through valleys of laughter, on rivers of peace,
In this map of connection, our worries release.

Each moment a treasure, a sight to behold,
Stories of love, like whispers retold.
In the warmth of shared dreams, we seek and we find,
An atlas of spirit, through hearts intertwined.

With every soft glance, our stories align,
Tracing paths of existence, where all souls shine.
In a world full of wonders, we share and we play,
The atlas of contentment, guiding our way.

So here's to the journey, both near and afar,
In the dance of the cosmos, we each are a star.
Embracing the movement, no shadow shall fall,
In the atlas of souls, we unite, one and all.

Petals of Positivity

In gardens where sunlight plays,
Each petal shines in gentle sway,
Whispers of joy in soft embrace,
They brighten up the dullest space.

With colors bold and scents so sweet,
They lift our spirits, light our feet,
A dance of love, a fragrant song,
In every heart, they help us belong.

When shadows loom and skies are gray,
Let petals guide us on our way,
For in each bloom, a spark we find,
A gentle nudge, a hopeful mind.

So gather up those petals bright,
Let them wrap you in warm light,
With every bloom, a chance to see,
The beauty in life's tapestry.

The Engineering of Euphoria

In the workshop of delight,
Blueprints written with pure light,
Screws of laughter, bolts of cheer,
Constructing joy that draws us near.

Wires of kindness, circuits spun,
Every heartbeat, a race begun,
With dreams as tools, we build our fate,
Creating wonders that vibrate.

Mechanisms of hope align,
A rhythm flowing, sweet divine,
The gears of love turn strong and free,
Engineering our harmony.

So let us forge, with hands entwined,
The essence of the heart combined,
In this grand workshop, we shall find,
Euphoria, a treasure blind.

The Spellbook of Cheerful Tidings

In ancient tomes where secrets dwell,
Words of joy weave their spell,
Pages filled with laughter's tune,
Awakening hearts like a flower in bloom.

A sprinkle of hope, a dash of grace,
Enchantments light up every face,
With chapters of kindness, verses of care,
Each line a promise, each word a prayer.

As wands of friendship wave above,
Stirring potions with threads of love,
This spellbook holds the keys to bliss,
Unlocking moments we dare not miss.

So gather round, come take a look,
Find your joy within this book,
For in each page, a world ignites,
With cheerful tidings, dreams take flight.

The Recipe for an Untroubled Heart

Begin with a cup of open mind,
Add a spoonful of love, refined,
A sprinkle of laughter, light and free,
Mix in the joy of simply being me.

Stir in kindness, a generous dash,
A hearty serving of memories to stash,
Blend well with the wisdom of days long past,
Creating a bond that's made to last.

Let simmer with patience, warmth, and grace,
A touch of serenity to hold space,
As gentle as whispers, as strong as art,
This is the recipe for an untroubled heart.

And when the time comes to share a slice,
Invite the world, be bold and nice,
For in every heart, this treasure lies,
A dish of love that never denies.

Weaving Wishes into Reality

In shadows, dreams take flight,
Threads of hope in golden light.
Each desire, a careful stitch,
Creating paths to reach the rich.

Fingers dance on fabric bright,
Weaving tales by day and night.
With every knot, a promise made,
Transforming wishes, unafraid.

The loom of life spins silently,
Crafting futures we can't yet see.
In every twist, a story flows,
Through trials faced, our spirit grows.

So let us weave with joy and grace,
Wishes bright in time and space.
For in this tapestry we share,
Lives entwined, forever rare.

Celestial Charts of Exhilaration

Stars align in velvet skies,
Whispers of the night arise.
Mapping dreams with every glance,
In their glow, our souls enhance.

Galaxies spin in wild delight,
Navigating through the night.
Feel the pulse of distant light,
Guiding hearts toward new heights.

Constellations tell our tale,
In their glow, we shall not fail.
Every twinkle, a kind embrace,
Chasing joy at a frantic pace.

So gaze upon the cosmic show,
In its beauty, let your heart grow.
Chart your course through endless dreams,
In the night, nothing's as it seems.

The Mosaic of Meaningful Moments

Fragments spark in daily grind,
Glimmers of joy, we seek to find.
Each small laugh, a piece so bright,
Building a canvas bathed in light.

Memories like tiles laid down,
In vibrant hues, no lack of crown.
Every hug, a gentle brush,
Creating art in life's soft hush.

Moments weave through time and space,
Each heartbeat, a sacred lace.
In the mosaic, stories blend,
A masterpiece that will not end.

So treasure each vibrant hue,
In life's gallery, it's all for you.
Collect the moments, big and small,
In this mosaic, we find it all.

Radiating Kindness

A smile shared, a gentle touch,
In this world, it means so much.
Ripples spread from heart to heart,
In each kindness, nature's art.

Sunlight breaks through clouds of gray,
Warming souls along the way.
Every word that lifts, inspires,
Nurtures hope, ignites our fires.

Tender gestures, small yet grand,
Create a strength that understands.
In the quiet, kindness reigns,
Soothing hearts and easing pains.

Together, let our spirits shine,
In every act, a love divine.
Radiating warmth through all we do,
Kindness blooms, forever true.

The Recipe for Elation

A sprinkle of laughter, a dash of mirth,
Mix joy with kindness, for all it's worth.
Stir in some dreams, let them rise and shine,
Serve with a smile, a taste so divine.

Add a pinch of hope, let it simmer slow,
Whip up some love, watch the flavors grow.
Share it with friends, let the warmth extend,
In every good moment, find time to blend.

Garnish with gratitude, that's the key,
Savor the happiness, set your spirit free.
The recipe simple, yet it fills the soul,
In each little bite, find yourself whole.

And when the days darken, and shadows play,
Cook up the elation, chase worries away.
For the secret lies not in what you seek,
But in how you cherish each joy unique.

Footprints on a Sunny Path

With each new step, the world awakes,
Golden rays dance on the whispering lakes.
Footprints behind show where I have been,
A journey of laughter, of loss, and of win.

The path stretches out, lined with bright trees,
Where the softest breezes carry sweet pleas.
Sunbeams flicker like fireflies at night,
Beneath the blue sky, everything feels right.

Each footprint a story, a memory made,
The sun on my face, all doubts start to fade.
Gather the moments, let worries dissolve,
In this sunny passage, life's puzzles resolve.

And as the day wanes, in twilight's embrace,
I cherish the wander, the light in my pace.
With every new dawn, I'll walk once again,
On sunny paths, where laughter has been.

Colors of a Cheerful Mind

In the canvas of thought, bright colors play,
A splash of red passion to brighten the day.
Yellow beams of sunlight, warm and alive,
In this vibrant palette, my spirit will thrive.

Swirling blues of calm, like skies up above,
Mix with greens of nature, a symphony of love.
Each hue tells a story, a feeling in bloom,
Crafting a world where the heart finds its room.

Purples of wisdom, soft whispers of grace,
Textures and tones create a sacred space.
Let colors surround you, let them unfold,
In the cheerful mind, treasures of gold.

For life is a tapestry, woven with care,
Each thread holds a dream, every color a prayer.
In the dance of the spectrum, find joy intertwined,
Embrace every shade of your colorful mind.

Melodies of Joyful Echoes

In the gentle breeze, a sweet tune flows,
Carrying laughter where soft music grows.
Each note a reminder of moments so pure,
Whispers of happiness, forever to endure.

The chime of the bells in the early morn,
Welcoming sunlight, a new day is born.
Melodies linger in the heart like a song,
Binding us together, where we all belong.

Songs of the birds in the branches above,
Filling the air with an echo of love.
Find rhythm in laughter, let voices arise,
In the symphony woven beneath open skies.

And as the night falls, stars join the choir,
Singing soft lullabies that never tire.
In the concert of life, let your spirit flow,
For the sweetest of melodies come from joy's glow.

The Garden of Glorious Moments

In the garden where laughter grows,
Sunshine dances, and the soft wind blows.
Petals whisper secrets, bright and clear,
In this sacred space, joy draws near.

Each bloom reflects memories we hold,
In hues of happiness, stories told.
Time stands still, a precious embrace,
In the garden, we find our place.

The Lighthouse of Joyful Adventures

In the distance, a beacon glows bright,
Guiding lost ships through the starry night.
With every wave, stories unfold,
In the lighthouse, dreams are bold.

Adventures await at every beam,
Chasing horizons, igniting a dream.
With laughter echoing through the air,
In joyful exploration, we dare.

The Scroll of Sweet Serenities

Unfurl the scroll of gentle peace,
Where worries fade, and troubles cease.
Words like whispers, soft and kind,
In every line, solace we find.

As twilight falls, stars begin to sing,
In the quiet, our hearts take wing.
Every moment a treasure so rare,
On this scroll, we breathe in the air.

Designs of Daring Delight

Textures and colors, a vibrant scene,
In daring designs, creativity's sheen.
Each stroke a spark, igniting the mind,
In the dance of creation, joy we find.

Adventures await in every idea,
Chasing the thrill, facing our fear.
In the tapestry woven with care,
Delight's daring touch, everywhere.

Recipes for Radiant Days

A pinch of laughter, bright and clear,
A sprinkle of joy to hold you near.
Mix in some kindness, let it blend,
Stir in hope, with love to send.

Sunrise whispers, painting skies,
Moments cherished, no goodbyes.
Dancing shadows, soft and warm,
Gather the blessings, embrace the charm.

Savor the sweetness, life's delight,
Catch the spark of purest light.
Share a smile, let spirits rise,
Each day a gift, a sweet surprise.

So fill your heart with colors bold,
In every story, let joy be told.
A recipe written, for hearts that sway,
In the radiant kitchen of each day.

The Almanac of Cheerful Discovery

Pages turned, adventures await,
Pathways leading to a golden fate.
Days of wonder, secrets unfold,
New horizons, treasures untold.

Nature's canvas, colors bright,
Guiding footsteps into the light.
Curious hearts, eager to roam,
Finding joy in every home.

Whispers of magic, breeze in the air,
Every moment, a chance to care.
With open minds, let journeys start,
Discovering beauty, a map to the heart.

In laughter's echo, wisdom sings,
In every heartbeat, a treasure rings.
The almanac shines, guiding the way,
To cheerful moments that never decay.

The Compass of Grateful Hearts

In the depths of stillness, gratitude grows,
A gentle compass that always knows.
Pointing to kindness, forever true,
Navigating love in all you do.

Silent moments, filled with grace,
Each heartbeat, a warm embrace.
Thankful whispers, soft and light,
In grateful hearts, the world feels right.

The stars align, guiding our way,
Count the blessings at the close of day.
With every breath, let gratitude start,
The compass leads to a thankful heart.

So cherish the journey, every part,
Follow your compass, trust your heart.
In the dance of life, take your place,
Filled with gratitude, a warm embrace.

Mosaics of Mirth

Colorful pieces, laughter's art,
Fragments of joy that never part.
Each smile a tile, carefully placed,
In the grand mosaic, moments embraced.

Threads of laughter, woven tight,
Creating beauty in morning light.
Every giggle, a joyful sound,
In this tapestry, happiness found.

Dancing shadows, swirling around,
In the gentle chaos, joy is crowned.
Together we build, with love as our glue,
A mosaic of mirth, vibrant and true.

So gather the pieces, let them shine,
In the artwork of living, twine by twine.
Celebrate the joy, let spirits lift,
In mosaics of mirth, we find our gift.

Building Blocks of Delight

In the garden of dreams, we play,
Collecting moments, bright as day.
Each laughter shared, a cherished block,
A tower built, beyond the clock.

Colors swirling in the sky,
Joyful whispers, hearts awry.
Foundations deep in trust we lay,
With every smile, we find our way.

Together we build, side by side,
In the glow of love, our hearts abide.
Step by step, we'll reach new heights,
With blocks of joy, we chase the lights.

Every challenge, a chance to grow,
In the dance of life, we ebb and flow.
With each heartbeat, we start anew,
Building blocks of delight, me and you.

Sketches of a Joyful Heart

With every line, my heart takes flight,
Sketching dreams in colors bright.
A canvas filled with love's embrace,
In gentle strokes, I find my place.

The laughter of a child nearby,
In every giggle, spirits fly.
Each moment captured, pure and sweet,
A joyful heart feels life's heartbeat.

With pastels soft, I draw the sun,
In every shade, our worlds are spun.
Together painting skies, so clear,
In sketches bright, I hold you near.

With every brushstroke, joy I see,
In the art of love, it's you and me.
Creating memories, a work of heart,
In sketches bold, we'll never part.

Echoes of Pure Bliss

Whispers of the wind softly sing,
Echoes of joy, in every spring.
Nature smiles, a gentle sway,
In pure bliss, we lose our way.

The sound of laughter fills the air,
Moments shared, beyond compare.
In every heartbeat, echoes flow,
A melody of love we know.

Fields of green and skies of blue,
In harmony, I dance with you.
With every echo, joy multiplies,
In pure bliss, our spirits rise.

Together we hear the world's sweet song,
As echoes of bliss carry us along.
In the stillness, let love persist,
In life's embrace, sweet echoes twist.

The Playful Dance of Gratitude

In the morning light, we sway and spin,
Gratitude blooms from deep within.
With every step, our hearts take flight,
In playful dance, we greet the light.

The joy of giving, a heartfelt play,
Thankful whispers guide our way.
In every twirl, blessings unfold,
As we dance together, brave and bold.

Moments shared, a gift so rare,
Gratitude's song fills the air.
With every movement, love we share,
In playful rhythms, we find flair.

Together we weave this vibrant thread,
A tapestry of joy, where love is spread.
In the dance of life, let's not forget,
Gratitude's joy is the sweetest duet.

Blueprinting Elysium

In dreams we sketch the skies,
A haven where hearts soar high.
Each line a whispered wish,
Crafting peace in a gentle brush.

Golden grains on fertile ground,
Seeds of hope and love abound.
With every stroke, we weave delight,
A paradise born from the night.

Mountains rise, with rivers flow,
Light illuminates, shadows go.
Together we build, hand in hand,
A blueprint drawn on sacred land.

Elysium calls, we take the leap,
Where dreams unfold and passions seep.
In unity, we find our way,
Blueprints guiding, come what may.

Portrait of a Merry Mind

Colors splash and laughter sings,
Joy is found in simple things.
A canvas bright, bold strokes collide,
Happiness becomes our guide.

Thoughts dance like sunlight's rays,
In a world of everyday plays.
Each moment paints a vibrant hue,
Creating life, alive and new.

With whimsy woven into dreams,
The merry mind finds vivid themes.
A portrait filled with warmth and cheer,
A space where love grows ever near.

In strokes of light, we trust and see,
A lively heart sets our minds free.
Radiant beams, our souls entwined,
Forever framed, a merry mind.

Echoes of Elevated Spirits

Whispers rise in twilight's grace,
Echoes dance in unseen space.
Spirits soar on twilight's breath,
Carrying love beyond the death.

In moments shared, our laughter finds,
A thread connecting all our minds.
Notes that shimmer, softly glide,
Uniting souls, like ocean tide.

Memory's embrace, a sacred song,
Reminds us where we all belong.
Through echoes, hearts are intertwined,
Elevated spirits, deeply aligned.

In every echo, every sigh,
We rise together, endlessly high.
In the realms where light abounds,
The spirit's echo knows no bounds.

Joy's Tranquil Terrace

On joy's terrace, peace resides,
A gentle breeze where love abides.
Sunset hues paint skies above,
A sacred space, a garden of love.

Each petal falls, a whispered prayer,
In nature's arms, we find our care.
Soft laughter mingles with the trees,
As time slows down upon the breeze.

In quiet moments, hearts connect,
A symphony of sweet respect.
With every breath, serenity flows,
A tranquil view where compassion grows.

Joy's terrace blooms, a vibrant scene,
Nurtured by hope, forever green.
In tranquil grace, our spirits rise,
A haven where longing never dies.

9 789916 882184